A Brother's
Little Instruction Book

GW01080976

A Brother's
Little Instruction Book

Jasmine Birtles

BOXTREE

First published 2000 by Boxtree
an imprint of Macmillan Publishers Ltd 25 Eccleston Place London SW1W 9NF
Basingstoke and Oxford

www.macmillan.co.uk

Associated companies throughout the world

ISBN 0 7522 7160 1

1 3 5 7 9 8 6 4 2

A CIP catalogue record for this book is available from the British Library.

Designed by Nigel Davies
Printed by Redwood Books, Trowbridge, Wiltshire

BROTHERS.

Who needs the brotherhood of man when being a brother is such an awesome responsibility? You have to help your sister find her true worth by selling her into slavery. And you have to teach your little brother social skills for life, like how to spit straight, where to find the best dirt and how to fart the national anthems of thirteen countries. It's a tough call, but with the aid of this book you'll have one-upmanship sorted at home and at school. And don't ask for thanks – ask for money.

You know you're an
unpopular boy
if you play hide and seek
and no one comes
to look for you ...

... and you stay hidden
for over a year.

Best thing about growing up:
the toys get bigger.

Worst thing:
you start paying for them.

As a brother,
you should always stand up
for your sister in social situations.
Lines like, 'Come on,
she's worth at least fifty quid,'
will always go down well.

Worry your sister.
Tell her she's looking really good.

Become an only child in one easy lesson.
Replace the sandpit with quicksand.

Top uses for a baby sister:
target practice
a magnet for other sisters you fancy
target practice.

Brothers-in-law
are often outlaws.

A brother is a bloke who hates the same people you do.

He ain't heavy, he's my brother. Yeah, only in space!

Don't let school interfere
with your education.

What time is it when you find your
little brother reading your diary?
Time to punch his face in.

What do you call a father
who never tells you off,
who helps you with your homework
and offers you money
even when you don't ask?
A stepfather.

Laugh and the world
laughs with you.

Laugh at your sister's boyfriend
and you'll have one testicle
hanging alone.

Start every day with a smile
and get it over with.

Tell your sister about
the birds and bees:
how to trap, kill and eat them.

Sisters are like mosquitoes –
always whining, often a pain
and they drink your blood.
No, wait!
That's vampires ...
sorry, no, it is sisters.

The best thing in the world
is to have a large, close,
loving family –
at least a hundred miles
from you.

You know you're unpopular
when even your imaginary friends
beat you up.

You know your little brother
has a bad attitude if he keeps
hitting you back.

The worst thing about
younger siblings is their tendency
to break your toys, mess your room
and lose your puzzles –
especially if it's at work.

Little sisters shouldn't
be allowed to have anything sharp
– like a mind.

Little sisters are better than
big sisters. They never do things
'for your own good'.

21

Offer to do
the washing up occasionally,
even when you haven't
done anything wrong.

How to get money
out of your parents:

whine

beg

inherit

sue.

 23

Rule of family life:
if at first you don't succeed,
NAG!

You're not your parents' favourite
if your brother gets a bike
and you get an egg-whisk.

If you want your sister
to do something for you
try using these three magic words:
'You're so thin.'

Try telling your sister she's really
pretty. She'll believe you once.

The worst things your sister can describe you as are 'sweet', 'potty-trained' and 'my husband'.

Brotherly love
= Brotherly loans.

Ideal birthday presents
for your sister:
Dreamcast, a Sony Playstation
and a year's subscription to Loaded.

... until she gives you My Little Pony,
mascara and a punch in the mouth.

As a brother
you shouldn't let anyone
insult your sister.
Haggle.
Get a decent price for her.

Older brothers
should set a good example,
but not too good.
No one likes to grow up
with a smart-arse.

What's the worst thing
about sisters?
Bovine spongiform encephalitis.
(This only counts
if she's a cow.)

Famous Brothers:
Noel and Liam Gallagher,
Gary and Martin Kemp,
President Assad of Syria
and the purple one out of
the Teletubbies.

Good birthday presents for your brother:
a Superman outfit (in your size),
a pair of trainers (in your size),
a babydoll dress and matching handbag
(in his size).

Note to Granny when sending
birthday cards: Dec-imal-isat-ion.

What you want for Christmas:
a model.
What you get:
a model aeroplane.

Don't let anyone be rude to your sister.
Get in there first.

Worst birthday presents
from your sister:
navel fluff, pretty pink underpants,
chicken pox.

When it comes to birthdays,
the thought doesn't count.

The best incentive to clean your room –
possible girlfriend.

Thirteen to eighteen.
Guess what? When you're a grunting,
acne-ridden idiot who can't dress
himself or tidy up – life is unfair!

Confuse your parents.
Ask them how they are.
And how things are at work and no,
I don't need any pocket money, thanks.

Find out what a frog in a blender
really looks like.

Does Samantha Janus
have a brother called Hugh?

Have a lock fitted on your wardrobe.
Your sister will want to
supplement her meagre
thousand-item clothes collection.

For some reason,
society has decreed that
your sister can wear your clothes
but you can't wear hers.
So redress the balance.
Steal her boyfriend.

Help your mother
round the house – play in the garden.

Annoy your brother.
Draw underwear
on the girls in his copy of Razzle.

Not only is Big Brother watching you,
but he's taken all your sweets
and he's mined your bedroom.

Don't play fair with your sister.
Tell her your friend fancies her
with braces and in her cagoule.

A brother is a machine
for blaming others.

Seven Brides for Seven Brothers?
Imagine what a stag night
that must have been!

If your parents tell you
you're getting a new little brother,
celebrate.
You can do to him all the things
your elder brother did to you.

 42

... The problem is,
you won't get away with it
like he did.

Jam miniature marshmallows
up your nose and try
to sneeze them out.

Did you hear about
the dyslexic brother and sister
who committed insect?

Are you your brother's keeper?
That depends which zoo you're in.

Things you have to
share with a brother:
parents, bedrooms, measles.

Less famous brothers:
Wayne van Gogh,
Keith Mandela,
Tarquin Capone,
Craig Einstein,
Ashley the Hun,
Trevor di Caprio,
Brian de Niro.

Separated at birth:
Hugh
and Russell Grant,
John F.
and Nigel Kennedy,
Kenneth
and Robbie Williams,
Tony
and Lionel Blair.

Ways to worry your parents:
tell them that they exist only
in your imagination;
ask them what gender they are;
cultivate a Norwegian accent;
stand over your father's shoulder
mumbling as he reads.

Younger brothers: proof that your
parents didn't learn the first time.

To err is human.
To have feathers and a beak is chicken.

Never keep anything
under your bed. That's the first place
your mum will look.

Don't envy your older brother.
Remember, he will go bald, get fat,
divorce and die first.

Help your sister find her true worth:
sell her into slavery.

Family values are never clearer than
when you're reading the will.

Always listen to your
little brother's problems.
It gives you something to
make your mates laugh later on.

Family values are great until you have
to pay tax on them.

Teach your little brother social skills
for life: how to spit straight, where to
find the best dirt and how to fart the
national anthems of thirteen countries.

A big-headed brother is one who thinks
he is everything you are.

Two is company,
three is bad birth control.

Do unto others
before they do it all over you.

Always put up with hand-me-downs –
unless it's fish-fingers and mash.

A bird in the hand
does it on your wrist.

Parental advice can be very useful
so long as it doesn't interfere
with your other plans.

Never trust a dog
to watch your food.

Never tell your mum
her diet's not working – not if you want
to continue to eat, anyway.

Playing with a vacuum cleaner and
a kitten at the same time could lose you
your pocket money for a year.

Great party tricks to develop:
sneezing with a mouthful of crisps
blowing lemonade out of your nose
armpit farts.

Never baptize a cat.

Don't pick on your little brother
when he's holding a cricket bat.

Laugh and the world laughs with you.
Tread on dog poo
and you'll stand alone.

One of the best things
about being a boy:
the world is your urinal.

Big sisters are like horoscopes:
they always tell you what to do
and they're always wrong.

Little brothers:
proof that evolution
can move in reverse.

Better safe than
punch your sister's boyfriend.

Children's books
your parents won't buy you:
The Children's Guide to Hitch-hiking,
Strangers Have the Best Sweets
and
Meet Dad's New Wife – Derek.

Books you should consider writing:
Puppies Can Fly,
Controlling the Playground
– Respect through Fear
and
Pop Goes the Hamster and Other Fun
Microwave Games.

If at first you don't succeed,
get new batteries.

Worry the family –
flush the toilet and go 'uh-oh'
in an urgent voice.

Strange and unnatural facts of life:
if you put a sandwich in a video
recorder it won't come up on screen;
Rod Stewart will never stop going out
with blondes a quarter of his age;
and your brother does
have a birthday too.

If you can't have your friends round
to play, dial 999. You'll get a new bunch
of playmates in fun uniforms.

Worry your parents.
Be quiet for at least an hour.

Little plastic ketchup packets make
really good 'blood squibs' for pets.

Practise making fax and modem noises
before your dad takes you
to his office for the day.

If your parents like children
to be seen and not heard,
always dress very loud.

Be a good loser but try not
to get too much practice.

Don't be afraid to speak your mind
but start to worry if you
have nothing to say.

You can get up in the morning.
It's just a question of
mind over mattress.

It's a big responsibility
to have a little sister –
so tell her she's a foundling.

Give your sister something
she'd really like for her birthday.
Leave home.

Tell your sister's new boyfriend
not to worry, her inexplicable rash
must have gone by now.

Curiosity killed the cat,
so why has it spared your sister?

If a family row breaks out,
don't pick sides.
Wait till you see who's winning.

Stand by your dad,
unless your mum's
throwing things at him.

You may be your own worst enemy
but only when your brother's not there.

Disturb your sister:
tell her you don't want anything for
your birthday because she's already
made your life complete.

Remember, your brother's
just another nut on the family tree.

If you can't sleep,
be sure to let everyone know.

It's good for boys to cry,
so do your brother regular favours.

Your brother will always look out
for you, so learn how to hide.

Tell your father
how strange it is
that you don't look like him
at all ...

... but you do look
an awful lot
like his best friend.

Excuses that won't get you off games:

The hamster ate my shorts

Running brings me out in a rash

I've got my period.

Names that could get you
kicked in the playground:
Tarquin,
Crispin,
Cecil,
Julian,
Jeffrey Archer.

Play soldiers with a difference.
Dip yourself in egg
and bite your legs off.

Stand-in teacher:
a moving target for darts,
ink-pellets and abuse.

Wear your bicycle helmet
all the time and tell people it's part of
your 'astronaut training'.

Your sister will always be with you,
but you can lose her in a crowd.

You can't make friends
without making mistakes.

Fast food is how it's cooked,
not how it's meant to be eaten.

Too many cooks spoil the broth,
so send out for pizza.

Help your brother with his hobby.
Beat yourself up.

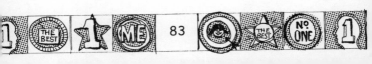

Remember, your sister knows
if she has a spot. She doesn't need it
circled with a felt tip.

Worry your older brother by
pretending to like his music.

If your brother's nice to you,
wonder what he's up to.
If he's very nice to you,
it's too late – he's already done it.

Don't ask for thanks, ask for money.

   85

There may be more than one way
to skin a cat but you won't be thanked
for finding out.

If your sister asks for a lift
tell her she's looking slim today,
then wave as you drive away.

Don't embarrass your sister.
She's capable of doing that for herself.

If at first you don't succeed,
get your parents to do it.

Your mum and dad will do
anything for you, but don't
expect them to do everything.

Don't make fun of your
sister's boyfriends unless they're
weaker than you.

Turn yourself into a real-life
Action Man – have a crew cut,
a realistic scar and no genitals.

Cool sandwich-filling idea:
peanut butter, jam, sausage,
Pringles and grated Mars bar.

If you must have a tattoo
get a temporary one.
But remember, they're not iron-on.

Always listen carefully
to your parents' advice
before rejecting it.

Activities that could get
you kicked in the playground:
embroidery
skipping
hopscotch
playing kiss-chase (in a boys' school).

Drive your father mad.
Say, 'Ooh, suits you, sir,' every time
he changes his clothes.

If you have a bad school report
show it to your mum while
she's on the phone.

You are not arrogant,
you simply have no reason to be humble.

Even if you don't know
which end of a girl is which,
you'll still be popular if you
fake an interest in her star sign.

When out at a restaurant,
remember, mange tout does not mean
eat everything at the table.

Drugs are for people
who can't face real fun.

You don't need to know any more
about politics than you see on the
Cartoon Network.

You're missing the point
if you sneak behind the bike sheds
to mend your bike.

95

You know you're an unloved child
if your mum wraps your lunch
in a road map.

You know your family's loony
if when the clock goes 'Cuckoo!'
they all take it personally.

Christmas: the time of year
when you get toys your
dad can play with.

Scientists have found a cure
for teenage angst.
It's called money.

 97

You're a teenager if you
can dress yourself but you can't
remember where you dropped
your clothes.

The thing about trouble is that
it always starts out as fun.

Don't bother being an early riser.
The telly's rubbish at that time of day.

Ways of earning extra pocket money:
paper round
doing jobs for your gran
blackmailing your dad about his mistress.

 99

Dads are good at biology and like to
teach you by asking trick questions like
'Do you think I'm made of money?'

Dads know everything there is
to know about football, until you start
playing it with them in the park.

If teachers are so clever,
how come they're the ones who have
a book with the answers in it?

School tests:
a fiendish adult ploy to find out how
much you don't know.

Follow your dad's example.
If you have spelling mistakes in your
homework blame your PA.

Be worried if you go to
a Halloween party and you win the
'scariest face' competition
– and you're not wearing a mask.

There's only one thing worse
than doing homework:
telling the teacher the next day
that you haven't done it.

You're in trouble if your
new teacher tells you she has
a black belt in teaching.

It doesn't pay to insult your dad.
He knows where you live.

You know you've got a lazy mum if,
on sports day, she sends
the au pair on the mother's
egg and spoon race.

Fathers work very hard
for their money. At least that's what
they'll tell you when you
ask them for some.

Don't run away from home.
Steal the car.

Let your dad help you with your homework. It might take longer but it'll make him feel wanted.

'Ooh, Mum, look at the new pet that's just come in!' is not a good response to your sister's latest boyfriend.

It's not a good sign
if your friends call your family meal
Biffo's Circus or Theatre of Death.

It's time to tidy your room when you pick
up an old comic and find a little brother
you never knew you had under it.

If you're a third child you were
only born so that your parents could get
the full worth out of the clothes.

You come from a frugal family
if your clothes are old enough
to vote but you aren't.

Good news: there is no Devil.
Bad news, there is no Father Christmas.
No news:
they're both just Daddy in disguise.

Your little brother's IQ
stands for 'Idiot Quotient'.

Don't complain about wearing your
brother's hand-me-downs.
It could be worse.
You could have had your sister's.

Put a warning sign on your family album:
Warning – may contain nuts.

Put-down for your sister:
'You're like medicine –
thick, bitter and hard to take.'

Put-down for your brother:
'I heard you donated your brain
to science and they gave it back.'

If it's slimy, hairy, ugly and
has lots of legs ...
it'll look great in your sister's bed.

In the school canteen,
table manners are a sign of weakness.

Stories you'll never hear at bedtime:
'The Care Bears Maul Some
Campers and are Shot Dead',
'The Boy Who Died from
Eating All His Vegetables'
and
'Postman Pat Goes Berserk with a
Machete in the Shopping Precinct'.

If you must spray graffiti
at least get the spelling right.
'Terry is a Wonker' doesn't quite work.

Give your parents time.
You'll be surprised at how much
they can learn in ten years.

Don't do a moonie
at the back of the bus
on your way to school.
Wait until the bus has stopped
so that more people
can benefit from the sight.

The spin cycle
on the
washing machine
makes cats dizzy ...

... The tumble dryer
is not a good place
to put your baby sister
when she's wet.

Phrases to drive your
sister bananas:
'Oh, are moustaches in fashion now?',
'No, you're not paranoid.
Everyone does hate you,'
and
'Someone does fancy you.
It's your games mistress.'

Apple-pie beds,
spiders in cupboards
and plastic turds on the carpet may
spook your sister
but if you really want to scare her
just look at her lovingly and ask:
'When, oh when, will I ever
meet a girl as sexy as you?'

Make the most of
all-you-can-eat buffets:

keep going back for more
and tell your parents it's because
you have multiple personalities
and have to feed them all

get more on your plate
by stamping down the lettuce with
your foot, and making a pyramid
with the carrot sticks

pull your chair over and eat
directly from the buffet.

If your gran gave you toiletries,
any type of figurine or anything
crocheted for Christmas
don't send her a thank-you note.
People with these sort of taste
disorders shouldn't be encouraged.

If you're forced to spend
yet another day playing with
your tedious cousin just smile at him
when you are alone and say,
'Did you know you're illegitimate?'

Rule of life:
if you find a girl
who can cook like your mother
she will look like your father.

Rule of life:
if you live on your own
you will never find a magic
laundry basket like the one at home
that manages to wash, dry,
iron and put away
all your dirty clothes.

If she's blonde,
slim and beautiful,
you're right,
you won't get anywhere with her.

Particularly if she's your sister.

We're all descended from
fishlike creatures but it
shows more on little brothers.

You're only young once
but you can be immature for
as long as your parents live.

Jasmine Birtles is a legend in her own surgically supportive lingerie. Her huge success in publishing has funded a high-rolling lifestyle of fast cars, rock star attention and a $3,000 a week coke habit. Actually it funded someone else to do all these things. Jasmine has had to make do with beans on toast and a three quid a week cocoa habit. Her one big luxury is at weekends when she switches on the other bar on her electric fire. Her hobbies include making scale models of ocean liners from discarded prosthetics and leg-waxing. She is not really interested in football so she supports Southend.